UNDERSTANDING ORGANIZATIONAL CHANGE

Converting Theory to Practice

Lynn B. Fossum

A FIFTY-MINUTE™ SERIES BOOK

CRISP PUBLICATIONS, INC.
Menlo Park, California

UNDERSTANDING ORGANIZATIONAL CHANGE

Converting Theory to Practice

Lynn B. Fossum

CREDITS
Editor: **Michael G. Crisp**
Designer: **Carol Harris**
Typesetting: **Interface Studio**
Cover Design: **Carol Harris**
Artwork: **Ralph Mapson**

Copyright © 1989 by Crisp Publications, Inc.
Printed in the United States of America

English language Crisp books are distributed worldwide. Our major international distributors include:

CANADA: Reid Publishing Ltd., Box 69559—109 Thomas St., Oakville, Ontario, Canada L6J 7R4. TEL: (905) 842-4428, FAX: (905) 842-9327

Raincoast Books Distribution Ltd., 112 East 3rd Avenue, Vancouver, British Columbia, Canada V5T 1C8. TEL: (604) 873-6581, FAX: (604) 874-2711

AUSTRALIA: Career Builders, P.O. Box 1051, Springwood, Brisbane, Queensland, Australia 4127. TEL: 841-1061, FAX: 841-1580

NEW ZEALAND: Career Builders, P.O. Box 571, Manurewa, Auckland, New Zealand. TEL: 266-5276, FAX: 266-4152

JAPAN: Phoenix Associates Co., Mizuho Bldg. 2-12-2, Kami Osaki, Shinagawa-Ku, Tokyo 141, Japan. TEL: 3-443-7231, FAX: 3-443-7640

Selected Crisp titles are also available in other languages. Contact International Rights Manager Suzanne Kelly at (415) 323-6100 for more information.

Library of Congress Catalog Card Number 88-72251
Fossum, Lynn B.
Understanding Change
ISBN 0-931961-71-8

This book is printed on recyclable paper with soy ink.

This book is dedicated to Cheney, Cory, and Jim
with thanks for their patience and support.

ABOUT THIS BOOK

UNDERSTANDING CHANGE is not like most books. It stands out from other self-help books in an important way. It's not a book to read—it's a book to *use*. The unique "self-paced" format of this book and the many worksheets encourage the reader to get involved and try some new ideas immediately.

The objective of UNDERSTANDING CHANGE is to provide the reader with a basic understanding of several major theoretical models of change and show how these models can be understood and applied to real-world situations. By applying the information presented, the reader will become a successful "change agent."

UNDERSTANDING CHANGE (and other titles listed in the back of this book) can be used effectively in a number of ways. Here are some possibilities:

—**Individual Study.** Because the book is self-instructional, all that is needed is a quiet place, some time and a pencil. By completing the activities and exercises, a reader should not only receive valuable feedback, but also practical steps for self-improvement.

—**Workshops and Seminars.** The book is ideal for assigned reading prior to a workshop or seminar. With the basics in hand, the quality of the participation will improve, and more time can be spent on concept extensions and applications during the program. The book is also effective when it is distributed at the beginning of a session, and participants "work through" the contents.

—**Remote Location Training.** Books can be sent to those not able to attend "home office" training sessions.

There are several other possibilities that depend on the objectives, program or ideas of the user.

One thing for sure, even after it has been read, this book will be looked at—and thought about—again and again.

PREFACE

Change is the only constant we live with. According to experts, 98% of all our knowledge has been accumulated in the last 50 years. The US Patent Office granted one million patents during the last fifteen years, compared to three million patents in the previous 175 years! Other countries are experiencing similar events. Worldwide, this represents tremendous **change** both in organizations and personal lives.

Has your company made a recent major change, reorganized, or relocated across town or across the country? Are you a manager or supervisor of a group affected by such changes? Managing change is no frivolous task. It is critical to the economic and emotional well-being of you and those in your organization.

You've probably heard the term "managing change." All good business schools now teach about the planning process. But what happens if you are past that point? If that is the case, this book should help. **This book isn't about planning for change that may happen. It is about coping with change once it has been decided and/or announced.**

This book will help you develop an overview of the process of change. It will help you look at change at all levels: personal, group, organizational and environmental. It will teach you basic principles of change and enable you to help your employees through the stages of change. *Understanding Organizational Change* contains ideas and activities you can use immediately with your employees.

Successfully managing change is a complex task. It is critical to your effectiveness as a manager in today's rapidly changing world. Those who are best prepared to understand and handle change will be the leaders. Good luck as you complete this book.

Lynn Fossum

TABLE OF CONTENTS

SECTION I

WHAT IS CHANGE?

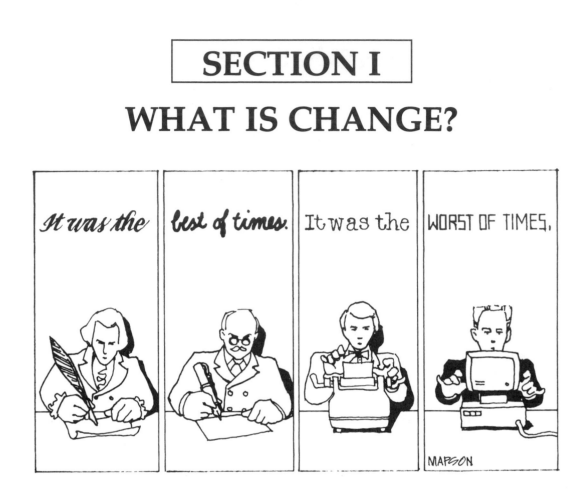

HISTORY AND PERSPECTIVE

Do you think of change as a new phenomenon? If you think about it, you will realize that change is and has been continuous since the beginning of time. For example, there are no longer dinosaurs or Vikings (except in museums). Even better, go to a library and look through some magazines from the 1950's. You will be amazed at how much has changed!

It is apparent that business, industry and even our homes have been highly affected by automation, computerization and new working conditions in recent years. New patterns of interdependence among governments, companies, unions, managers and individual workers are emerging. We are truly becoming a world community.

Change has affected policies, procedures, rules and roles. All have been led by changes in management and organizational philosophy. Many readers have probably witnessed a transition from a more authoritarian style of management, to either management by objective, or increasingly "participative" management. Examples of participative management include quality circles—developed in Japan and instituted in several countries including the United States with the International Association of Quality Circles, EI—Employee Involvement (developed at Goodyear), and PRIDE—People Responsibly Involved Developing Excellence (developed at IBM) among many others.

In progressive companies it is apparent that today's workers represent a different profile from those appearing in the assembly-line operations of previous generations. The authoritarian manager and hierarchical management structure that served those organizations are no longer effective for today's increasingly service and information directed society. Today's jobs are different and workers' ways of functioning in their jobs are different. In progressive societies, workers are better educated, more expensive and in shorter supply for skilled positions.

Not all change requires that people believe in what is being changed, only that they get it implemented. The pace of rapid change today, however, forces organizations to reevaluate their beliefs about the change process. Forced change, without workers' support, will result in a half-hearted, inefficient operation.

HISTORY AND PERSPECTIVE
(Continued)

> *The stress of change can be positive. Change encourages innovation.*
> *Preparing yourself for innovation and responsiveness to change is essential.*
>
> *Lynn B. Fossum*

CASE IN POINT

The Inertia Company was bought by an outside group when the founder, Ploddius Stagnant, decided to retire. The new buyers saw an excellent opportunity to take advantage of Inertia's basic product line by expanding into markets not previously developed under Stagnant's direction. The production and operations procedures were immediately revamped and upgraded. The new management brought in the latest techniques from their MBA programs. They enthusiastically purchased and installed new equipment, developed new procedure manuals, revamped operations and established different inventory controls. Production declined. They revamped the manuals, reviewed the operations and rearranged the equipment. Production declined further. What happened? Why?

(Write your thoughts in the space provided below and compare them with those of the author on the facing page):

Here is what I think happened:

MANAGERS AS CHANGE AGENTS

Traditional management training focused on learning the basics of planning, organizing, delegating, monitoring and controlling. However, as a manager these days, you probably spend less time on the traditional management functions and more time in roles such as conflict-resolver, resource-allocator and information-disseminater.

In all probability, you have not had much management training in your role as a change agent. Most managers who have not been so trained, approach change by using the most common directive management role—that of an advocate or salesperson. We say these individuals have a "tell and sell" approach to change.

Most managers assume that a problem is solved when employees verbally agree to a change. Later this manager may learn that the employees have neither accepted nor learned how to implement the change. This was exactly what happened in the situation described in the Inertia Company case on the facing page, *namely the employees didn't support the change.*

Do not mistake verbal agreement for behavioral implementation. In today's complex world you have a new managerial function and challenge—facilitating change. It is time to learn how to develop your skills as a change agent. This is what the remainder of this book will help you accomplish.

> **A working definition of change:** "Change in an organization essentially means a modification of the way things get done in the system"

ROLES IN ORGANIZATIONAL CHANGE

During any change process, there are three important roles that people fill. Decide which best describes you and check the appropriate box:

1. ☐ **Change Sponsor**—these are individuals or groups with the power to determine that a change will occur. *Change sponsors* legitimize the change by sanctioning or decreeing it...In most organizations a change sponsor is usually upper level management.

> You are a change sponsor whenever you are the person initiating a change.

2. ☐ **Change Agent**— these are individuals or groups responsible for seeing that a previously determined change occurs...This is normally the role of middle and lower level management.

> You are a change agent when it is your job to implement the change in your group.

3. ☐ **Change Target**— these are individual or groups who are asked to change something (knowledge, skill, attitude or behavior) as a result of the change...This is normally a workgroup. As a manager, it is your job to assist them in adapting to the change.

> You are a change target when *you* must add new skills or are asked to undergo change.

It is possible to occupy different roles during the process of change. This book however, will focus primarily on the tasks of the change agent, recognizing that at times your role may also include being a change sponsor and/or a change target.

YOUR POSITION

Before we can help others respond to change we need to understand or clarify our personal feelings. Take the time right now to determine what change signifies for you by responding to the following statements:

When a major change comes my way, I:

☐ Can express my feelings about what's happening

☐ Can discuss it with my family and friends

☐ Learn what my co-workers think

☐ Will realistically assess what will happen in my job because of the change

☐ Can decide whether to support the change or sabotage it

☐ Also do the following:

_____

_____

_____

Change can occur in two ways. Somtimes it is your choice to make a change; it is a change that you choose. Sometimes a choice is made for you by others; it is a change that chooses you. Frequently a person's attitude about a change is determined by the degree of choice (and control) they have about the change. Is this true for you?

CHANGES YOU CHOOSE

If you are like most managers, when you perceive a need your normal action is to recommend or initiate changes. These are "changes you choose" and before announcing them you should evaluate several factors including:

1. What is the authorization agreement between you and your boss

   _____ Does your boss expect you to check with him or her first? or

   _____ Does this person want you to initiate change and bring in the results after the fact?

2. What style of leadership do you feel you and your boss exhibit most of the time? See definitions on page 23, and then rank you and your boss with a "1" for most like and a "5" for least like:

You	Your Boss
_____ Task Leader	_____ Task Leader
_____ Impoverished Leader	_____ Impoverished Leader
_____ Country Club Leader	_____ Country Club Leader
_____ Middle of the Road Leader	_____ Middle of the Road Leader
_____ Team Leader	_____ Team Leader

3. Can you identify the significance of the change in the following areas?

   How much it costs?

   What parts of the organization will be affected?

   How extensive the change will be?

   Who will be personally impacted by it?

4. Do you have the necessary courage and stamina to implement the change?

CHANGES THAT CHOOSE YOU

Occasionally a change may be announced by your superiors that you may question. This is a change that "chooses you." After you question the change with your superiors and receive clarification, if you still disagree with the change, you have several choices, including:

1. Insist higher management is wrong and attempt to convince them to change their position.

2. Carry out the change with as much enthusiasm as you can muster.

3. Carry out the change but complain to your subordinates that it is a mistake.

4. Leave the organization.

    In this difficult situation, remember two key objectives of any manager:

- **To contribute to the effectiveness of the organization**
- **To develop team support and maintain high morale**

If it is impossible to do both from a change that "chooses you", you need to do some serious thinking about your future with your current organization.

Whether it is a change that you choose, or a change that chooses you, as manager you need two kinds of skills:

Product or Technical skills—which make you a content expert in your specific field, e.g. engineer, machinist, computer programmer etc. These skills provide the technical know-how to make a change work.

Process skills—which make you an expert at knowing what process to use with people so that they can accomplish a specific goal e.g., problem solving, decision making, and so on. These are the people-skills that a manager uses to help people implement change.

THREE KEY SKILLS

There are several key process skills which will help you successfully manage change. The most important are *empathy, communication* and *participation.* Be sure you understand each of these processes and how to use them whenever you act as a "change agent." Following is a brief definition of each:

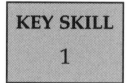

KEY SKILL

1

Empathy—This is the ability to understand where the others are coming from *without being there yourself* (i.e., to be able to "put yourself in their shoes"). To do this you need to understand those you will be involved with in the change. What motivates them? What is happening to them personally?

To improve your ability to understand perspectives other than your own consider the following questions:

✔ What would I be thinking now if I were facing this change?

✔ What would happen to my job because of this change?

✔ Would my status be affected?

✔ How are my basic priorities affected by the change?

✔ How would my work relationships be affected?

THREE KEY SKILLS (Continued)

| KEY SKILL |
| 2 |

Communication—This allows you to effectively create understanding about who, what, when & how things are occuring. For an excellent book on how to improve your interpersonal communication skills, read *The Art of Communicating* by Bert Decker.*

Remind yourself that all communication involves a sender, a message, and a receiver. For effective communication, all three elements must be in play.

Following are some questions to consider when communicating about change:

To communicate this change

☐ Which is better, oral communication or written communication? _____

Why? _____

☐ Was my message clearly communicated? _____

How do I know? _____

☐ Was there an opportunity to communicate about the change

at the right place? _____

at the right time? _____

in the right way? _____

☐ Did I receive effective feedback? _____

☐ What are my next steps? _____

---

*To order *The Art of Communicating,* use the list in the back of this book.

THREE KEY SKILLS (Continued)

KEY SKILL 3

Participation—in 1948 Lester Coch and John R.P. French, Jr. conducted a study about resistance to change. Their setting was a clothing factory where they experimentally controlled minor changes in work procedures (communicated by 4 different management methods). They recorded the problems of resistance which arose. Their conclusion: *Resistance to change could be best overcome by getting those involved in the change to participate in its implementation.*

In 1960 participative management existed in very few organizations. By 1970 books on participative management were beginning to proliferate. The Japanese approach to participative management in the form of quality control circles grew throughout the 1970's and has gained international acceptance. Today the International Association of Quality Circles, based in the U.S.A., is currently expanding its activities to many types of participative management approaches.

As a manager of change, (i.e., a change agent), you can encourage employees to participate in the change process by asking them to:

- appraise their own performance

- schedule their own time

- design improvements in the work flow

- assist in the decision making

Repeated studies have shown that when employee participation is encouraged during change, the payoff is increased motivation and reduced negative behaviors such as slowdowns and failure to comply with standards. Check that on your bottom line!

SECTION II

THEORETICAL MODELS

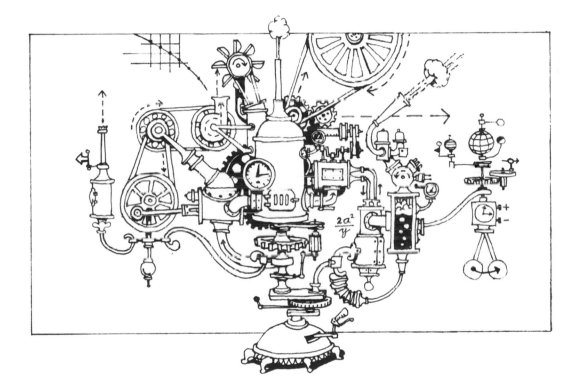

THEORETICAL MODELS

Studies have shown that if people are trained only in techniques, without understanding the theory behind these techniques, they cannot easily apply them to anything beyond a specific situation. The factors and variables that contribute to change management are too complex to memorize a few simple techniques that can be applied to any change situation.

This section will provide you with an understanding of several theoretical models of change. These models include:

- **Force Field Analysis (Kurt Lewin)**

- **Configurational Learning**

- **Gap Analysis (Delta Analysis)**

- **Innovative Change**

- **Leadership Intervention**

- **NACA**

- **Systems Theory**

- **Pendulum Swing**

- **Grief Cycle**

Later, you will also find a model to use when asked to choose which change techniques would be most effective in a given situation. Combining the above theories and techniques will help you manage change more successfully.

MODEL 1:

FORCE FIELD ANALYSIS (Kurt Lewin)

Kurt Lewin is generally regarded as the "father of change theory." It was he who developed the first model of the change process in the late 1940s. He called his model "Force Field Analysis" to support his concept that change was represented by the pressure of opposing forces acting on a situation.

In applying Force Field Analysis, it is important to begin with a definition of the problem. This is frequently in the form of a question, e.g., "Why can't we change the way we work together?"

The next step is to identify the factors or pressures that strongly support change in the desired direction. These are called the *driving forces* and are diagrammed as arrows pushing upward. Similarly it is important to identify those factors or pressures which are obstacles to change. These are known as *restraining forces* and diagrammed as arrows pushing downward.

The current circumstance (situation) is the middle line. The relative strength of each of the various forces is shown by the length of its line. When behavior in a group or organization is stabilized, the forces pushing for change (driving forces) are equal to the forces against change (restraining forces). Lewin's exact term for this dynamic balance of forces was "quasi-stationary equilibrium" (Q-S equilibrium).

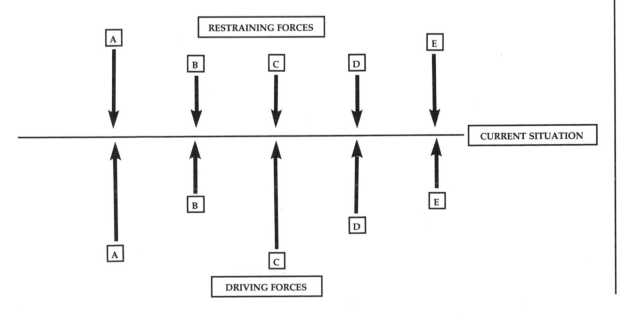

FORCE FIELD ANALYSIS MODEL (Continued)

✔✔TECHNIQUE TO USE

For change to occur, the balanced forces in "Q-S Equilibrium" must be changed by:

(1) strengthening or adding driving forces,

(2) removing or reducing restraining forces, or

(3) changing the direction of some of the forces.

Take this opportunity to think of a situation in your organization where Lewin's theory could be demonstrated. Begin by identifying a change being instituted in your organization. Briefly describe it in the space provided:

_____

_____

_____

Assign strength to each force on a scale of 1(low) to 10 (high):

☐ List the driving forces:

_____ _____

_____ _____

_____ _____

_____ _____

☐ List the restraining forces: Weight (1-10)

_____ _____

_____ _____

_____ _____

_____ _____

FORCE FIELD ANALYSIS MODEL (Continued)

If change occurs only by adding or strengthening driving forces, the change being introduced may result in increased tension. This tension (as will be seen later) often reduces effectiveness. Tension can usually be minimized by removing or diminishing restraining (opposing change) forces. This also contributes to a more stable change since old restraining forces which have been removed will not remain to push for a return to old behaviors and ways.

☐ Identify four ways to remove/reduce the restraining forces:

_____

_____

_____

_____

Changing the direction of some of the forces is one of the most efficient ways to obtain change. When it is possible to turn restraining forces into driving forces often everyone can "win". This is best done by testing the assumptions underlying the force, clarifying outcomes, and recognizing the resulting benefits.

☐ Identify four specific ways to change direction of your forces:

_____

_____

_____

_____

FORCE FIELD ANALYSIS MODEL (Continued)

Lewin's model sees behavior change through three phases: unfreezing behavior, movement within positions, and refreezing behaviors. To unfreeze a behavior, an individual or organization must become uncomfortable enough with the old way to want to try something new. After the movement phase (implementing the actual change), the final step is to "refreeze" the new behavior or attitude. This occurs when a manager provides adequate rewards, compliments, and/or encouragement for the person adopting the new response. Ultimately, this person comes to see the response as reflective of his or her own needs and preferences.

☐ What kinds of rewards, compliments and encouragement could/did you provide during a recent change?

Employee	Reward	Compliment	Encouragement
_____	_____	_____	_____
_____	_____	_____	_____
_____	_____	_____	_____

MODEL 2:

CONFIGURATIONAL LEARNING

Each of us is guided by language patterns and previous experience when we select what to perceive, how to interpret it, and how to organize it. This is called a *configuration*. For example, a person raised in the U.S. Midwest refers to a flavored, carbonated soft drink as "pop" and sparkling water as "soda". Upon moving to the West Coast they are met with looks of confusion when ordering "pop" instead of "soda". They must redo their *configuration* so that "soda" is now the term also used for flavored, carbonated soft drinks.

Each configuration is our decision of what to ignore and what to attend to in a total context. We are usually unaware of doing this. Thus when things appear to be static, we think we must make them change. "Social change", "organizational change" or "previous change" is really a reference to changing what only *appears* to be a static condition.

Configurational learning is the natural process that occurs when an individual's previously determined configurations change. This process involves *rearranging, adding to, subtracting from,* and *re-evaluating* previous configurations. Configurational learning acknowledges that the natural activities of interpreting and organizing are in fact the same as "changing". It encourages an appreciation of the process rather than attempting to force something that occurs anyway.

While each person's configuration organizes him or her for action, at the same time it restricts the formation of alternative actions. Thus, in creating a configuration of the world as stable and therefore manageable, the awareness of natural change is blocked out.

CONFIGURATION LEARNING MODEL (Continued)

However, when a configuration is no longer useful, a person may become bored and begin seeking new approaches and opportunities—ie., change. The drive for change can occur in several ways. A few include:

1. The ability to block out awareness of a change is incomplete and the realization of the new condition is confusing. When the old configuration fails often enough to take note, a person begins seeking new alternatives.

2. The current configuration may appear wrong or self-defeating. The resulting uncomfortable feelings then instigate change.

3. Crises may occur. These are usually times of the most dramatic configurational learning. Sudden insight into problems may occur (often referred to as an ''Aha, now I understand'' experience). On a more modest level a configurational rearrangement may be more the realization of a reduction in discomfort.

   These crisis experiences often form the milestones in our lives.

✓✓TECHNIQUE TO USE

☐ Can you identify circumstances in which you or your organization had an ''aha'' experience? List them below:

_____

_____

_____

_____

☐ What were the outcomes?

_____

_____

_____

_____

MODEL 3:

GAP ANALYSIS (Delta Analysis)

Delta (Δ) is the Greek symbol for difference, or change. In Gap Analysis, change is seen as converting the way things are now to the way we want things to be.

The process of defining the difference between two states, identifying the steps necessary to get from "the way things are" to the "way we want to be," and implementing the steps is seen as change. In real life, the gap or difference is less visible. The process can be portrayed as two circles as illustrated below. The circle on your left is labeled 'the way things are now'. The circle on the right is labeled 'the way I want things to be'.

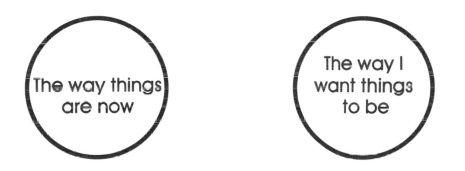

Now, bring these circles together and allow them to partially overlap (as shown in the diagram below). Usually we like some of the "way things are now", and in moving to what we "want things to be", desire to preserve some of the present. That is what the overlap portrays.

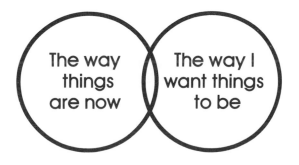

GAP ANALYSIS MODEL (Continued)

Complete the following Gap Analysis for current change in your life.

The Way Things Are	The Way I Want Things to Be	Steps to Get There

MODEL 4:

INNOVATIVE CHANGE (Nolen and Nolen)

There is a difference between creativity and innovation. *Creativity* looks at options and generates ideas* *Innovation* takes an idea and develops it into a practical application. Innovation requires some change in *behaviors, processes* or *functions:*

Nolen and Nolen suggest the following 8 step model for innovation. Check those which you use when you need to innovate.

I try to:

☐ 1. Acknowledge the desire/need to innovate

☐ 2. Clarify the opportunity to innovate

☐ 3. Generate innovative ideas

☐ 4. Select the ideas most likely to succeed

☐ 5. Firm up the idea/vision

☐ 6. Perform a Gap Analysis

☐ 7. Develop action and contingency plans

☐ 8. Implement the action plan

Steps 2-5 are important for protecting the process of innovation from environmental stress. Steps 6-8 prepare the environment to foster innovation.

---

*For an excellent book on this topic, order *Creativity In Business* by Carol Kinsey Goman using the list in the back of this book.

INNOVATIVE CHANGE MODEL (Continued)

✔✔TECHNIQUE TO USE

Now take a change you wish to implement through the Eight Step Innovative Change Model by answering the following questions in the space provided:

1. We need to innovate because _____

2. These are our opportunities to innovate: _____

3. Innovative ideas: _____

   _____

   _____

4. Ideas most likely to succeed: _____

5. Our most firmed up idea: _____

6. Our Gap Analysis

The Way Things Are	The Way I Want Things to Be	Steps to Get There
_____	_____	_____
_____	_____	_____
_____	_____	_____
_____	_____	_____

7. Our action plan from the Steps to Get There:

Action	Initiation/Completion Date	Who Will Do It
_____	_____ / _____	_____
_____	_____ / _____	_____
_____	_____ / _____	_____
_____	_____ / _____	_____

8. How we will implement our action plan:

MODEL 5:

LEADERSHIP INTERVENTION MODEL
(Blake & Mouton)

Robert Blake and Jane Mouton devised a model of managerial leadership and change. Their thesis is that five definite styles of leadership emerge. Each can be described by defining how individuals orient themselves with regards to *concern for task* and *concern for people*. These assumptions underlie how leaders intervene. They provide important clues to your leadership style as a change agent.

1. **TASK LEADER**—A person who is primarily concerned with a task. People in this category are viewed only in relationship to their contribution to the task. The role the "task leader-change agent" takes is to plan, direct, and control the behavior of people because the assumption is that most people are basically lazy, indifferent and irresponsible.

2. **IMPOVERISHED LEADER**—This individual avoids involvement and emphasizes neither other people, nor the task. The "impoverished leader-change agent" role is to tell people the expectations and let them decide what to do because the assumption is that no one can really change another person.

3. **COUNTRY CLUB LEADER**—This person emphasizes people and minimizes the task. This is because the main concern of the "country club leader-change agent" is with interpersonal relationships. This change agent's role is to make sure people are not upset no matter what happens to the task.

4. **MIDDLE OF THE ROAD LEADER**—This individual seeks satisfactory and workable solutions by seeking balance and compromise. The underlying assumptions value traditions, precedent and social conventions. The "middle-of-the-road leader-change agent" seeks consensus before implementing change.

5. **TEAM LEADER**—This person has maximal concern for both people and the task. The underlying assumption is the interdependence of people. The "team leader change agent's" role is to involve people and their ideas to determine the strategies and conditions used to achieve the task.

LEADERSHIP INTERVENTION MODEL
(Continued)

✔✔TECHNIQUE TO USE

Which leadership style best describes you?

☐ Task Leader

☐ Impoverished Leader

☐ Country Club Leader

☐ Middle-of-the-Road Lead

☐ Team Leader

Provide a personal example of your choice in the space provided below:

_____

_____

_____

_____

Did it work? _____

Would another style have been successful? _____

Why/Why not? _____

_____

_____

_____

If not, what can you do to learn additional skills and styles?

_____

_____

_____

_____

MODEL 6:

NACA (Notice, Attitude, Choice, Action)

People respond to change in both an emotional and intellectual change cycle termed NACA:

First they must **Notice** that a change has or is about to occur.

Next they must develop an **Attitude** about the change by gathering data and setting priorities.

The next step is to **Choose** to support or resist the change.

Finally they can take **Action** on their choice.

Very often a person will understand the need for a change from a practical, intellectual point of view. For example, moving to another state to accept a promotion is an excellent career change. But there may be upset feelings (emotions) about the change, no matter how much sense it may make. In the above example, the change (move) means giving up friends, feeling alone, leaving a favorite home, etc.

What often happens is that the NACA change cycle occurs at different rates at the emotional and intellectual levels. While a person may well be intellectually ready to take **action** (they *think* it's a great idea), their emotions may still be at the **attitude** stage (it *feels* awful to give up friends). This splits the level of commitment and often produces mixed messages. The result is confusion. It is important to learn to distinguish the difference between deteriorating commitment and the confused communications people make when "their heads are willing but their hearts are lagging."

NACA MODEL (Continued)

✓✓TECHNIQUE TO USE

Who are the ''Heads Willing'' on your team?   What stage are their hearts?

_____   _____

_____   _____

_____   _____

☐ Is anyone's heart ahead of their head?

☐ What does this tell you about the NACA cycles?

HEART SIDE OF THE BRAIN

HEAD SIDE OF THE BRAIN

MODEL 7:

SYSTEMS THEORY

In general systems theory, an organization is seen as a complex system with boundaries allowing input and outgo. This system exists within a larger external environment that is constantly exerting pressure on its boundaries, an environment with which the organization must interact.

Systems theory recognizes that a change in one part of the system often creates change throughout the system. If one part changes, other parts must change to accomodate the new situation. Change in a system can have a domino effect. A common example of system theory is the expression, ''a chain is only as strong as its weakest link.''

The organizational system, defined by its boundaries and internal structures, is considered relatively stable. The external environment is assumed to be in a state of continual flux. For example, a purchasing department (a part of a manufacturing system) orders 1000 widgets each month from the same vendor (in the external environment). When the outside vendor increases prices, the system begins to change. To maintain profits, manufacturing must reduce labor costs by changing production methods, or research must develop a product without widgets, or purchasing must find another vendor, or finance must pass along the price increase, etc. Sometimes many or all of the mentioned changes may occur.

As described in the example above, change occurs when there is a significant discrepancy between the organization's output/input and the demands of the environment. When the discrepancy is minimal, the system is stable. When the discrepancy is great, the system must change.

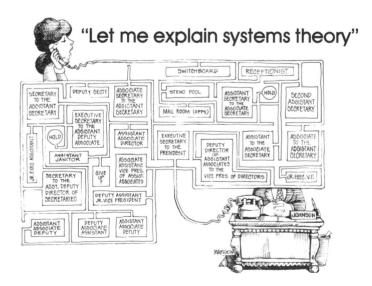

"Let me explain systems theory"

SYSTEMS THEORY MODEL (Continued)

✔✔TECHNIQUE TO USE

CASE STUDY

> The management and employees of the International Institute were deeply saddened by the unexpected sudden death of President and Chairman of the Board, Heldin S. Teem. Because of the significance of his position, an international search for a successor was undertaken. An interim president, well known and respected, was appointed from the current management. Months after Mr. Teem's death, employees were far behind on important projects and several had tendered resignations. A general air of uncertainty and low commitment prevailed.

What change happened in the system? _____

How might it have affected other parts of the system?

    Research & Development: _____

    Sales & Marketing: _____

    Finance: _____

    Manufacturing: _____

    Operations: _____

    Personnel: _____

How might stability be restored?

_____

_____

_____

_____

How has change created a disruption in the system you work in?

_____

_____

_____

MODEL 8:

PENDULUM SWING (Beverly Gaw)

The pendulum swing represents the learning theory of *overcompensation* or *overlearning*. Ineffective, polarized behavior—both old and new—is discarded as new behaviors are learned, practiced, and incorporated into a person's behavior pattern.

During the change process it may be disconcerting to be at the sending or receiving end of pendulum swing behavior. You have probably felt the pressure of this swing. For example, your secretary may have just attended an assertiveness seminar. The first day back, you receive an emphatic ''no!'' to your request for a cup of coffee.

Eventually, the new assertive behavior is comfortable, fits the situation, and becomes fully a part of the secretary. You may now be pleasantly told that getting you a cup of coffee immediately interrupts his or her work schedule. However, if you would like to wait until there is some free time, you will receive your cup of coffee.

The pendulum of functioning has moved to a higher level. The new response is neither habitual (said automatically) or specifically planned (rigid and rehearsed for the situation). Rather it is a spontaneous response to a situation. The response is flexible and accommodating to the circumstances—and a lot easier to be around.

PENDULUM SWING MODEL (Continued)

✔✔TECHNIQUE TO USE

☐ Make a list of people on your team who are in a pendulum swing:

_____

_____

_____

_____

_____

_____

_____

Observe their responses for a week. Then determine what part of the pendulum swing they are in. Record in this space:

Person		New Learning	Practice	Incorporated

MODEL 9:

GRIEF CYCLE (Elizabeth Kubler-Ross)

As a physician working with cancer patients, Dr. Elizabeth Kubler-Ross saw her patients, their families and the care-givers who worked with them progress through a predictable cycle of grief. All of her patients, their families and care-givers were facing a major loss; either their death or the death of a loved one. And all people seemed to undergo a similar transition, although at different paces and with differing degrees of intensity.

The initial stage was one of denial—choosing to believe that nothing major was really happening. The second stage was anger and outrage—how dare this be happening to them! This stage was usually followed by a plea-bargaining stage—making promises to God if the situation could just be changed. Frequently, those involved switched back into anger, expressed by depression or a sense of hopelessness and helplessness. The final stage was a form of acceptance, an awareness of the circumstances and a desire to do what was necessary.

Dr. Ross found that the cycle repeated itself as people wrestled with their circumstances. They continued to re-cycle as they coped with the grief and loss. Fortunately the cycle reduced in intensity over time. Frequently her patients came to a position of peace with themselves, long before their families accepted the probability of death.

This same cycle has been observed to occur for persons facing other types of loss. Loss can occur not only with negative events such as a divorce or being laid off, but can also occur with positive events such as a marriage or a new job. The common factor is *change*. Change creates a feeling of loss as people are required to give up old behaviors and patterns to adopt new ones.

GRIEF CYCLE MODEL (Continued)

✓✓**TECHNIQUE TO USE**

In the spaces below, list employees who might be experiencing a loss and identify their position in Kubler-Ross's grief cycle. Note if they are in the initial cycle or are re-cycling:

Employee	Loss	Stage	
		Initial	Recycle

_____

_____

_____

_____

_____

_____

_____

WHAT STAGE OF THE GRIEF CYCLE ARE YOUR EMPLOYEES IN?

REVIEW OF CHANGE MODELS

To review your understanding of the various change models define in your own terms the following

Organizations look at and respond to change through the following models:

- Force Field Analysis: _____

  _____

- System Theory: _____

  _____

Individuals respond to change mentally and emotionally via the following models:

- Configurational Learning: _____

  _____

- Leadership Intervention: _____

  _____

- Pendulum Swing: _____

  _____

- Grief Cycle: stage (1) _____   stage (2) _____

  stage (3) _____

These models explain steps that are taken during the change process:

- NACA: _____

  _____

- Gap Analysis: _____

  _____

- Innovative Change: _____

  _____

SECTION III

THE CHANGE MATRIX©
A working model

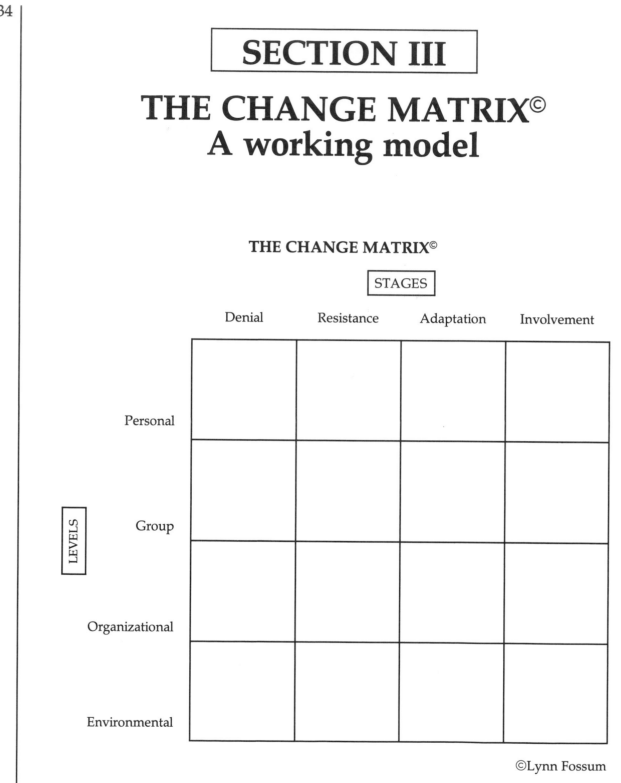

THE CHANGE MATRIX©

©Lynn Fossum

THE CHANGE MATRIX©

It is time to put the nine models from the previous section into a framework that can help you guide yourself and others through the process of change. Your goal is a successful implementation of any change for which you are responsible.

A BRIEF REVIEW

Let's briefly review the nine models:

Systems Theory and Kurt Lewin's **Force Field Analysis** provided general overviews of how organizations look at and respond to change. Lewin identified opposing and resisting forces for change existing within a system. System Theory identified limits and boundaries which keeps things relatively stable. However, a disruption in the system will cause change to occur.

Configurational Learning, Leadership Intervention, Pendulum Swing, and the **Grief Cycle** discussed how people respond to change mentally and emotionally.

Gap Analysis, Innovative Change, and **NACA** suggested specific steps to take during the change process.

To put all of these models in a working framework it is necessary to view change in two dimensions. The first dimension describes the **level** at which change occurs in a system. Change can occur for a person; a group; an organization; or on a very large scale of the environment. The second dimension describes the **stages** that are passed through in the process of coping with change. These stages are denial; resistance; adaptation; and involvement.

©Lynn Fossum

LEVELS OF CHANGE

Change always occurs for an individual, no matter what the level. However, the levels of change describe the *circumstances*, in which the change occurs. The levels are:

- personal

- group

- organizational

- environmental

PERSONAL CHANGE

There are times when change must be viewed at the **personal** level, because it affects the individual directly. For example, if your organization is making a major move to a distant city, the individuals who accept the move face major personal changes. There will be an upheaval of their family life, the loss of co-workers who do not move, a separation from friends, etc. These types of change are of major personal consequence. To help your employee cope with such a change you must address the personal impact the change will have upon that person. Reviewing the various models, especially the Configurational Learning Model, Pendulum Swing Model, and Grief Cycle Model, will give you additional insights. Those theories and techniques can provide a foundation for assisting your employees, co-workers, (and yourself) to cope with personal change.

GROUP CHANGE

If your particular **group** is moving to another office building in the same city, individuals will not be making a major personal change such as being uprooted from their homes in a move to a distant city. They may still discover, however, that they are facing a major change. Their work group may change, their assignment may change, their office arrangement may change, their commute may change, etc. The social or intragroup connections that they used before are no longer the same. Because the **group** is facing similar circumstances, many of their concerns are similar. As a manager you will need to assist them as a group.

LEVELS OF CHANGE (Continued)

Review the **Configurational Learning, NACA** and **Force Field Analysis** Models which will help you with group change. After you have done this:

☐ Identify two specific forces affecting your group:

    1. _____

    2. _____

☐ Are they restraining or driving forces? _____

☐ How can you change the group configuration to convert them to driving forces? Write your response in the space below:

☐ Do you notice the NACA theory operating in your group?

☐ Are some people ready to implement change before others are ready?

☐ What can you do to bring them into the same operating level?

LEVELS OF CHANGE (Continued)

ORGANIZATIONAL CHANGE

Perhaps your company has just merged with another. Individuals are now faced with an **organizational** change. New procedures, new policies, new culture and new people are all changes to be expected. In this type of change you must work cooperatively with many other people within the organization. While you will still have responsibility to assist your group in making the changes, you will also have responsibility to the entire organization's transition.

The models to review during organizational change include the **Innovative Change Model, Leadership Intervention Model,** and **Gap Analysis.**

☐ Assess the Leadership Styles of the managers you interface with.

What Leadership Style do you associate with:

Manager A _____

Manager B _____

Manager C _____

☐ Do you need to modify your style to accomplish change in your organization?

☐ If so, in what ways can you do that?

☐ What parts of the Innovative Change Model and Gap Analysis Model can you use at your next Manager's meeting?

ENVIRONMENTAL CHANGE

The final level at which change can occur is **environmental**. At this level, a change may be caused by a major political action such as new tax legislation. Or it may occur because of heightened awareness of a problem, such as toxic waste disposal. Environmental change requires implementation by organizations, groups and individuals. As a manager, this change will most directly affect you by its impact upon your organization. If you understand the **Systems Theory Model** and **Force Field Analysis Model** you can better anticipate and prepare for the changes that will occur.

LEVELS OF CHANGE

personal—

    group—

        organizational—

            environmental—

THIS IS NOT THE BEST WAY TO MANAGE CHANGE

STAGES OF CHANGE

It does not matter at what level change is occurring, there is a series of stages, or *phases*, that will be encountered in implementing the change. While the length of time spent in each stage may vary, each will occur while coping with change. The stages are:

- denial
- resistance
- adaptation
- involvement

STAGE #1: DENIAL

The initial stage is one of **denial**—a belief that nothing major is occurring, or if it is occurring, it won't affect me/us anyway. This stage is very brief for some people, and prolonged for others. At the group level this stage frequently takes the form of failure to recognize the group's part in the whole, e.g., an increase in the cost of widgets won't affect our jobs here in quality assurance. Failure to begin "blending" activities following an acquisition is an example of denial at the organizational level. During the denial stage your major task as a manager is to begin *building awareness* of the impact of the change.

STAGE #2: RESISTANCE

Denial is usually followed by **resistance**. Resistance can take various forms, ranging from a negative attitude to out-and-out opposition. It can even include sabotage of the change through work slowdowns, illness, irritability or sloppy performance. The stage of resistance can occur at any level. It is usually the most difficult stage during change. Your major task in successfully managing change during the resistance stage is *conflict resolution*.

STAGES OF CHANGE (Continued)

STAGE #3: ADAPTATION

Following resistance, the third stage is **adaptation**. In this stage the change begins to become accepted, and sometimes even welcomed. People learn to develop methods to implement the change effectively for themselves and others. During the adaptation stage, your managerial tasks become *goal setting and problem solving*.

STAGE #4: INVOLVEMENT

The final stage is **involvement**. In this stage individuals actively participate in the change, make contributions and suggestions, initiate work on their own, and come to see the change as the ''way it is''. Once the change is implemented and accepted things become stable again. It is during this stage that your managerial task of *team building* can begin.

STAGES OF CHANGE

denial——>>resistance——>>adaptation——>>involvement

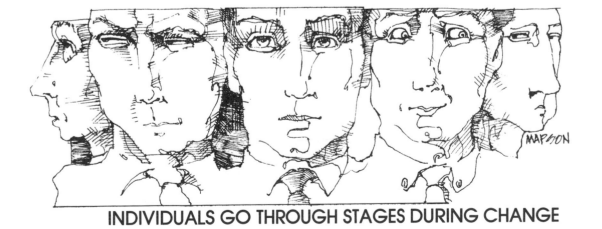

INDIVIDUALS GO THROUGH STAGES DURING CHANGE

THE CHANGE MATRIX©

THE CHANGE MATRIX©

STAGES

	Denial	Resistance	Adaptation	Involvement
Personal				
Group				
Organizational				
Environmental				

LEVELS

©Lynn Fossum

With the **Change Matrix©** you now have a method for identifying where each of your employees, in the change process. On the accompanying page is a Change Matrix© containing examples of phrases and comments you might hear regarding a specific change at that level/stage of change. Listen for similar phrases among your employees.

Section IV will provide more details about the various stages/levels of change and teach you techniques to use to assist people regardless of what stages or level they are in. But first you need to learn to use the Change Matrix© to assess your employees' positions in the change process. Directions for using the Change Matrix© are provided on page 44.

CHANGE MATRIX© EXAMPLES

STAGES

	Denial	Resistance	Adaptation	Involvement
Personal e.g. move to new office building	"No big deal. I've moved lots of times."	"How can I possibly do my work in a building with bad lighting!"	"If I move my desk over 3 feet and rearrange the file cabinet, I'll be much more efficient."	"My new office is really a boost to my morale. Adding plants and pictures make it a great place to work."
Group e.g. new boss	"Our new boss is perfect. She's not going to change a thing."	"We've been here longer. Our new boss doesn't know how our department operates. In time, she'll come around. Wait."	"Maybe the boss's new idea is a good one. How can we make it work here?"	Wow! This new procedure is fantastic. We really know how to do our job well!
Organizational e.g. budget cuts	"R&D is critical; they'll never change our funding."	"If they think they can expect any great products out of here after this, forget it."	"Dividing into individual tasks and meeting weekly might get the project out on schedule."	"This department-based plan for meeting the product deadline is right on target. What teamwork in developing it
Environmental e.g. tax law revision	"They'll never change the tax laws on real estate. The lobby is too powerful."	"This is hopeless. Forget about all real estate investments."	"Let's look and see if we can come up with any new angles."	"We're making our 3rd offering on rehab properties for low income housing. What a great investment opportunity this is!"

LEVELS

ASSESSING EMPLOYEES ON THE CHANGE MATRIX©

Begin by selecting an individual employee. Follow down the left side to determine at which level change is occurring for that person. (It is not uncommon for people to experience change at several levels.) Now follow across that row to the column showing the stage of change for that person. Put the person's name in the box where the column and row intersect.

Repeat this for each of your employees.*

THE CHANGE MATRIX©

	STAGES			
LEVELS	Denial	Resistance	Adaptation	Involvement
Personal				
Group				
Organizational				
Environmental				

©Lynn Fossum

USING THE CHANGE MATRIX© (Continued)

The Change Matrix is a tool which can help you determine where to focus your activity in successfully managing change. By looking at where your employees cluster, you can determine those methods that will be most helpful to you and your employees. Section IV will give you several activities to use during the **stages** of change: dealing with *denial,* removing *resistance,* allowing *adaptation,* and increasing *involvement.* By utilizing the knowledge and techniques in Section IV you can tailor your activities to effectively work with the varying **levels** of change: *personal, group, organizational,* and *environmental.*

It is important to recognize that the **level** of change may vary for each person, according to his perception, or *configuration.* Likewise, each of your employees will move through the **stages** of change at their own pace. Your challenge will be to support them through the process, while at the same time meeting the needs of your organization for continued production and service.

USE THE CHANGE MATRIX© WITH YOUR EMPLOYEES

*Lynn Fossum, 1989

SECTION IV

USING THE CHANGE MATRIX©

The Change Matrix© is a tool for you to use to identify the status of individuals who are making a change. You can use it to plot the locations of the various persons in your workgroup. Observing where the largest number of employees cluster will assist you in determining appropriate methods to help them through the change. You can also make accommodations for those who are in different **stages**/**levels** of change. The Change Matrix© is a tool to diagnose the change status of your employees.

This section will give you methods for dealing with *denial*, coping with *resistance*, encouraging *adaptation* and increasing *involvement* at the four levels of change: *personal, group, organizational* and *environmental*. In the process, you will be successfully managing change.

THE CHANGE MATRIX©

STAGES

	Denial	Resistance	Adaptation	Involvement
Personal				
Group				
Organizational				
Environmental				

LEVELS

©Lynn Fossum

USING THE CHANGE MATRIX©

By adding the levels of change,

LEVELS OF CHANGE

personal—

group—

organizational—

environmental—

+

At the stages of change,

STAGES OF CHANGE

denial——>>resistance——>>adaptation——>>involvement

---

you will end up with The Change Matrix©

	STAGES			
LEVELS	Denial	Resistance	Adaptation	Involvement
Personal				
Group				
Organizational				
Environmental				

DEALING WITH DENIAL

Denial is an amazing psychological defense mechanism. It is the coping skill that initially numbs us to changes we do not wish to acknowledge such as death or grave disappointment. It is the avoidance of acknowledging a situation while your internal resources gather themselves to cope. During the denial stage you frequently hear people say, "I really don't see that this is such a big deal", when in fact, it *is* a big deal. Or you may hear, "That decision isn't going to affect us anyway, so why worry?" or other similar phrases that indicate a lack of awareness of the consequences of a change.

RECOGNIZING DENIAL

If you find your employees refusing to acknowledge a major change, or seemingly unaware that things are or will be changing, it is a good bet that they are in denial. Later, after they have progressed through the other stages of change—resistance, adaptation, and involvement—their initial comments like "nothing big is happening" may be accurate. But right now, without passage through the other stages, it is probable that comments of "no problem", "what's the big deal?", are symptoms of *denial*, the first stage in coping with change.

Do you recall the first stage in Elizabeth Kubler-Ross's grief cycle? Or the initial stage in the NACA process, *noticing* that a change is occuring? Or the Configurational Learning concept of selectively choosing what to pay attention to? These are all references to the coping mechanism of denial.

RECOGNIZING DENIAL (Continued)

Unfortunately, "ignorance is bliss" does not help long when the change occurs. Your challenge as a change agent is to move your employees through the denial stage so they acknowledge the change and can begin their journey to become productive.

During the denial stage, the techniques and methods you use are intended to *develop an awareness* that a change is about to occur or has occurred. Until this awareness happens (along with an acceptance of its consequences), then preparation for the later stages of involvement and commitment cannot occur.

While overcoming denial and developing an awareness of the change, there may be confusion. Confusion at this stage can diminish adequate preparation for and understanding of the change. Take the necessary time to develop awareness and understanding. Don't rush this step, because understanding allows a person to move to the next stage which is resistance, normally, the most difficult stage.

DIFFERENTIATING DENIAL AND RESISTANCE

The denial stage may produce a lack of awareness or confusion. This is not the same as resistance. Resistance occurs only after a negative judgement of the change has been generated. Resistance requires some understanding of the change and occurs only after the denial stage has passed. There are many reasons for resistance. These will be discussed in the next unit. However, your first job is to break down the denial to develop an awareness that changes are occurring.

The activities on the next page should be helpful in developing an awareness for your employees that change is occurring. These activities can be used successfully during meetings where the changes are being discussed. They should be used selectively depending on your personality, the size of your group, and the depth of the denial.

ACTIVITIES FOR DEALING WITH DENIAL

✓✓**TECHNIQUE TO USE**

Select activities that seem most appropriate to the personalities of your group.

(check those you plan to use)

I plan to deal with denial by,

☐ **Taking a playful or adventurous attitude:**

Stand on the ''magic change carpet''—and explain the changes thoroughly.

Put on a police officer's cap and give the group the new operating procedure. Think up your own: _____

☐ **Encouraging the group to become more aware:** Ask, ''What can you tell me about the changes we will be facing?''

Record the answers on a chartpad visible to the group.

☐ **Redirecting the group's attention:** Ask, ''How is the change thus far versus how you imagined it would be?''

Record the answers on a chartpad.

☐ **Clarifying the ambiguity:** On a chartpad list responses to:

I like/ I don't like (about the change)

It creates these problems/ it solves these problems:

Add your own: _____

☐ **Creating ownership of the change:** On a piece of paper ask group members to complete the phrases about the change

''I believe the change will. . .

''I believe you believe the change will. . .

''I want the change to. . .

''I fear the change will. . .

''I understand why the change occurred because. . .

WORDS TO THE WISE

It is not uncommon for managers to overlook or rush the denial stage. Part of this comes from an eagerness to ''get on with it''. However, denial is a critical stage in coping with change. Unfortunately, your employees will pass through it at different speeds. This can cause frustration and confusion for everyone.

Some employees in your group may be ready to start planning. Others may seem dazed or out of touch. Your job is to respect everyone's style and pace while coping with change. In education, experienced teachers use an individualized approach to account for differences in learning speeds. You may find yourself needing to apply the same individualized approach in your group.

While you are dealing with denial, your goal must continue to be getting as much assistance and cooperation as possible while announcing the changes. Later on during the resistance stage, you may look back at this stage and wish again for the blissful unawareness expressed by some employees. Keep your perspective and sense of humor. Everyone will get through the stages of change in his or her own time.

**SOMETIMES IT IS DIFFICULT
TO RECOGNIZE DENIAL**

DEALING WITH RESISTANCE

The resistance stage of change is probably the most difficult stage—*for you and your employees.* The reasons for resistance are complex. The dynamics of how resistance gets expressed at the personal, group and organizational level are complicated. As a manager you need to give considerable attention to this stage of change.

During the resistance stage, several major issues emerge which you and your employees must face. These issues include:

- control/power/helplessness—a feeling there is no choice
- loss/grief—a feeling an important part of life is being lost
- risk—a feeling that the change brings danger
- conflict/anger—a feeling of a need to lash out at someone

Because these issues usually emerge during the resistance stage, you need to understand them and be prepared for their appearance.

CONTROL/POWER/HELPLESSNESS

The usual method that managers use during a change, is to convince or persuade the employees what a wonderful benefit it will provide for them. This is known as the ''tell and sell'' technique. However, if your employees are in the resistance stage, they will rarely be receptive to your message.

Often they don't want to hear about benefits. They feel their world has been turned upside down and they have lost control. At this stage, even the greatest reasons why a change may be of benefit will not make sense. It does not fit the employee's configuration. (See Model 2, Configurational Learning, page 17)

LOSS/GRIEF

Change is often perceived as a personal loss and therefore, is resisted. People fear they will be giving up a part of themselves to make certain changes. Although this may seem unusual considering it is a change in the work environment, consider that approximately one-third of the day—and half of our waking hours, are spent at work.

CASE STUDY

> A security study at a software firm recommended a change in the physical layout of the reception area. The reception desk was moved to a different angle and Missy Barnes, the receptionist, was given a revised greeting procedure. Her manager, Marge Jones, soon discovered she had an uprising on her hands. Not only was Missy upset, so were all the people who had to pass her "gate". Missy's formerly cheerful greeting had been replaced with a growl and a frown. Did she misinterpret the new procedure? Why do you think she was resistant to the change? Was she feeling a loss of control?

RISK

Risk taking behaviors vary from person to person because a risk is not something which is absolute. Risk is behavior which is *perceived* as either approaching or crossing an accepted boundary. In our interpersonal relationships we frequently err on the safe side. We imagine the boundary to be more restrictive than it is.

DEALING WITH RESISTANCE (Continued)

RISK (Continued)

Regarding risk, people's decision-making styles can be crudely classified into two types TYPE I people want lots of data, are low risk takers and try to protect themselves against public mistakes. They are careful, cautious, and prefer clearly defined tasks to challenging jobs. In trying to protect themselves from making an error, TYPE I people normally commit "Sins of Omission". They are reluctant to risk taking action.

TYPE II people are higher risk takers. They see the world full of possibilities, chances, resources and challenges. They view things in terms of what is possible, rather than what needs to be avoided. Those who commit TYPE II errors normally commit "sins of commission". They jump right in and take action.

How people approach risk is helpful in determining their response to change.

☐ Identify your employees as: TYPE I   TYPE II

_____   _____

_____   _____

_____   _____

_____   _____

_____   _____

☐ Does anyone fall in between?

TYPE I or TYPE II?

CONFLICT/ANGER

When a painful event occurs in an unaccustomed setting, people frequently feel angry. Very often resistance takes the form of visible conflict and tension. There are several ways of dealing with this conflict and some are more effective than others.*

Some of the primary ways to deal with anger are:

1. **Denial or withdrawal**—if we don't acknowledge the event, maybe it will go away. The problem is that it won't. It usually grows to an unmanageable stage that must be dealt with. However, when the issue or the timing isn't critical, denial may be a productive short term way to deal with conflict.

2. **Suppression or Smoothing over**—Pretending "things are always great" does not recognize the positive aspects of openly handling conflict. While the source of the conflict may not disappear, suppression may be the resolution when it is more important to preserve relationships than deal with *insignificant* conflict issues.

3. **Power or Dominance**—Unfortunately this is frequently used to settle differences. It always results in winners and losers. Usually the losers do not support a final decision with the same enthusiasm the winners do. In fact, they may sabotage future implementation with a conscious or unconscious renewal of the previously resolved struggle. In very large groups where other forms of handling conflict are inappropriate, power may be the most workable solution. Voting on a local referendum and "the resulting law" is an example of using power or dominance.

*For an excellent book on this subject, order *Managing Disagreement Constructively* using the list in the back of this book.

CONFLICT/ANGER (Continued)

4. **Compromise or Negotiation**—This sometimes encourages both sides to take an inflated position so there will be something to ''give'' later. It frequently results in a watered down solution with little commitment from anyone involved. Yet when resources are limited or it is necessary to avoid a win-lose solution, compromise/negotiation may be the best choice.

5. **Integration or Collaboration**—This occurs when all parties recognize the *contribution, abilities* and *expertise* of the others. The emphasis is on the group finding an optimum solution rather than defending a particular position or faction. The entire group's effort should exceed the sum of individual positions. The best of the group's thinking and commitment will emerge as everyone modifies initial views while the work progresses.

☐ Identify the individual Contributions, Abilities and Expertise of your employees in the space provided:

Employee	Contribution	Ability	Expertise
_____	_____	_____	_____
_____	_____	_____	_____
_____	_____	_____	_____
_____	_____	_____	_____
_____	_____	_____	_____
_____	_____	_____	_____

UNDERSTANDING RESISTANCE

What happens when people resist? Have you ever been around a two year old child? When angry, they just dig in their heels. They do not move, do not budge and do not cooperate. Most adults are different. Sometimes the worst part about a non-cooperative adult at work is that they PRETEND to cooperate. We call this passive-aggressive behavior.

Passive-agressive behavior is one of the most difficult types of resistance to deal with because it often *appears* that the person is doing nothing to interfere with progress. It's akin to engaging in a boxing match in a windowless room with the lights turned off. If a person is ''passive-aggressive'', you don't know where that individual is coming from. You don't know how to draw him or her out and you can't aim your punches, or anticipate from where your opponents attack will come.

A passive aggressive employee who resists change, often claims to be doing nothing. Sometimes that is exactly what they are doing, work included; but often energy is directed to sabotage, back-stabbing, griping, or bad-mouthing. It is important in coping with resistance to recognize that it is one thing to appear to comply; it is something else to actually comply.

THIS IS **NOT** PASSIVE-AGGRESIVE BEHAVIOR

SYMPTOMS AND SOURCES OF RESISTANCE

The symptoms of resistance to change in an organization can take many forms in addition to passive-aggressive behavior. Some symptoms, such as reduced productivity, might be attributed to factors other than resistance. When this occurs, time and money can be wasted on the wrong "cure". If a change is occurring in your organization, be especially sensitive to the following symptoms of resistance to change:

- Reduced productivity

- Poor work quality

- Increased absenteeism

- Slowdowns or strikes

- Increased number of grievances

Can you list more? _____

_____

_____

_____

Change can sometimes shift a person's status or reputation in a group or organization. People highly respected before the change because of their skills, longevity, experience, etc. may be brought to par with newcomers who have new skills or unique experience. This may add to the resistance of the change by "oldtimers" who have influence in the group. It is important for you as a change agent to be sensitive and aware of this and other sources of resistance to change.

SOURCES OF RESISTANCE (Continued)

The following list suggests sources of resistance to change. Put a check by those you feel may be present in your organization:

☐ The proposed changes appear to violate values/ethics

☐ Inertia already exists in the system

☐ The proposed changes represent uncertainty

☐ A misunderstanding of proposed changes is evident

☐ There is a fear of loss

☐ Personal antagonism exists among group members

☐ There is a lack of confidence in the change sponsor/s

☐ There is a lack of confidence in the change agent/s

☐ There is a lack of participation among team members

☐ There is a failure to see the need for the change

☐ The timing is very poor

☐ There is a disruption of social relationships

☐ The proposed changes could upset power balances

☐ Informal organizational pressure against the change is possible

☐ There is the belief that the change is a form of criticism about the way things have been done.

☐ There is the perception that benefits may result if there is strong resistance to change

Add your own:

☐

☐

What can you do about the sources of resistance that you have identified?

_____

_____

_____

_____

_____

ACCEPTANCE OR RESISTANCE TO CHANGE?

While *change agents* and *change targets* often do not have strategic roles in deciding change, they will, by their acceptance or resistance, decide the level of support given to implementing the change. This level of support eventually determines the success of the change.

PREVENTING RESISTANCE TO CHANGE

"An ounce of prevention is worth a pound of cure." And so it is with change. By creating and maintaining a climate that is receptive to change, much resistance can be avoided.

It is important to freely discuss changes as soon as possible. Rumors, grapevines, or third-party media releases lessen your credibility and lower trust of employees. Sincerity and open-access to you are critical during times of change. The more optimistic you feel about a change, the more optimistic your colleagues and employees will feel. The signals you send out will reflect your attitude and influence others. And during the heavy times, a sense of humor helps lighten the load.

If the developmental process of building commitment to change is not accomplished well, forced compliance will occur. With forced compliance will come resistance. If this happens, remember that resistance is not always a negative occurrence. It can bring to the surface problems to solve that help overcome unaccounted-for difficulties in the change process. Prolonged, however, unacknowledged resistance is costly. Lowered production, slowdowns, absenteeism, high turnover and poor morale are a few of the results.

RALLYING RESISTANCE

Too often resistance has a perceived negative value and therefore, managers traditionally attempt to use three essentially low-yield strategies to deal with it. Have you ever tried any of those listed below?

I have attempted to:

YES   NO

☐   ☐   1. Break down resistance by threat, coercion, bribery or reasoning.

☐   ☐   2. Avoid resistance by deflecting it, not hearing it, or creating guilt for expressing it.

☐   ☐   3. Discount resistance by dismissing it as unimportant, non-traditional, or non conforming.

YES   NO

☐   ☐

Were you happy with the results?

Resistance is a way for a person to protect himself or herself from overload or harm. It is thus a positive attribute of self-defense. Therefore, it should be recognized as an asset and accorded certain status. Resistance always exists when people perceive things to be contrary to their self-interest. Once this is understood, then resistance should be respected for what it is; i.e. self-protection.

In dealing with resistance, you must be quite clear about what you want from the resister. Be specific when communicating with the resister. Provide specific timeframes, outcomes, potential benefits, concrete behaviors, etc., and then approach the resistance positively through the four steps shown on the next two pages.

4 STEPS TO RALLY RESISTANCE

RALLY RESISTANCE (Continued)

Four Steps to Rally Resistance

1. Surface the resistance:

a. Make it safe to express resistance by assuring that the resister will not be attacked, punished or scolded.

b. Ask to hear all aspects of it and listen carefully without interrupting. This can be painful, but it is necessary to prevent working in partial ignorance.

c. After hearing all of it, ask clarifying questions to make sure you understand the concerns.

2. Honor the resistance:

a. Listen carefully and attentively. Listening is a real skill.* Make no attempts to interrupt, state your position, sell, reason, or imply the resistance is invalid while it is being explained.

b. Acknowledge the resistance by affirming the resister's right to resist. You do not have to agree, you *do* need to acknowledge it. Saying, ''I understand that you could feel concerned'', or, ''I see how that could be a problem for you'' are methods of acknowledging the other person's resistance.

c. Continue to make resistance safe by reinforcing the concept that it is safe to resist. Periodically state that resistance has value and the resister is appreciated for stating her opinion.

---

*For an excellent book on this subject, read *The Business of Listening.* To order, use the list in the back of this book.

3.   Explore the resistance:

a. Differentiate between authentic resistance and pseudo-resistance. Pseudo-resistance, while real, has nothing to do with the change. Instead it is rooted in old grudges, resentment of authority, need for attention, etc. Distinguish which is which by asking, ''What is *your* objection?'' Deal with the causes of pseudo-resistance later unless it is blocking progress.

b. Look deeper at the resistance by asking, ''What would you prefer?'' The resister then begins to work with you toward the objective rather than against it. The development of an agreement-intended change can be an outcome of this probe.

4.   Recheck the status of the current resistance and any agreements that have been made around it.

Remember, the objective is not to eliminate all resistance. This is not possible. Instead the objective is to reduce needless resistance enough to allow the change to continue to progress.

When the resistance is at a workable level, give acknowledgment to the resister with a thank you and move on. It is not necessary that the resister like the change and abandon all resistance. It is enough that the resister is willing to agree to it and begin acceptance of the change.

''The use of a cup is in its emptiness''—*Buddhist saying*

COPING WITH CONFLICT

Frequently, resistance will flame into open conflict. Most persons dislike or even fear anger and conflict that is openly expressed. However, an open expression of disagreement is the healthiest path to resolve a conflict. Despite common belief, when an emotion is experienced and fully expressed, it tends to be forgotten. It is the emotions that are not expressed or experienced that cause continuing pain and attract attention.

When conflict is not given room for expression and resolution, it does not disappear. It goes underground and remerges in disguised forms and non-productive ways. One way to bring conflict to the surface is to ask, during a meeting, that each person take sides on an issue. This will assist group members in confronting and clarifying their own positions about the change. Conflict resolution is a critical part of successfully managing change during the resistance stage. To learn more about coping with conflict, read *Managing Disagreement Constructively.* *

There is a considerable difference between disruptive conflict and constructive conflict. It requires managerial finesse to remove the options for disruptive conflict. Disruptive conflict occurs when there is a competitive climate within the organization. Stop and think—what happens when a defender on a sports team attacks his own teammate? This is akin to a competitive climate *within* the organization.

---

*To order *Managing Disagreement Constructively,* use the list in the back of this book.

In this climate employees perceive that the disagreement is a game in which some persons must lose so others may win. Stop and observe. Are your employees using such defense mechanisms as aggression, withdrawal, repression, projecting blame onto others, or deadlocking? If so, it is time to quickly move in to redefine the task and take away the competition.

Constructive conflict occurs in an atmosphere of high team spirit and commitment to group goals. Disagreements stem from a sincere involvement with the common problem. Stop and observe. Are these indicators of constructive conflict apparent in your employee group's conflicts about the change? Check those you have personally experienced:

☐ Discussing differing ideas you will come to an agreement as a group that is better than any one individual's initial suggestion.

☐ A genuine belief that your employees trust each other to be fair.

☐ Observing group cohesion (the sense of togetherness and belonging) as employees reach a solution they are all a part of.

As manager, it is a ''difficult reality'' to assist your employees during the resistance stage. The reality is that often the anger about the change and the resistance to it are directed at you. Avoiding the trap of needing to seek and obtain personal approval is a challenge you must face during this stage.

ALLOWING ADAPTATION

The third stage of change, **adaptation** occurs when your employees develop an understanding of the change *and* reflect a positive perception about it. (Resistance is shown by expressions of negative perception of the change.) During adaptation employees develop a sense of autonomy, or self-direction. They regain a sense of control over their destiny. Their acceptance of necessary change is increased, and implementation of the change begins. During this stage *goal setting* and *problem solving* become important processes for successfully managing change.*

To help employees move out of the resistance stage into the adaptation stage, you need to encourage:

- independence

- personal responsibility

- acceptance of differences

> Change usually occurs from the inside out. It occurs at different rates for different individuals.

ENCOURAGING GROUP ADAPTATION TO CHANGE

The following suggestions will hasten your group's adaptation to change. Check those ideas you can use to help your employees. I can:

☐ 1. **Encourage creative thinking.*** This can be self motivating. Creativity can often generate more efficient and effective ways of conducting business and implementing a change.

☐ 2. **Encourage employees to set their own goals for success.** People are more committed to that which they personally decide. They subconsciously seek ways to meet their own wants and needs. They become self-motivated.

☐ 3. **Set up an employee self-appraisal performance system.**** Ultimately such a system will result in greater employee responsibility, self-regulation, and motivation.

☐ 4. **Encourage different employees to conduct meetings.***** This reduces "group think", and enhances ownership and participation of team goals and objectives.

☐ 5. **Leave the room** if you feel that your presence is distracting or influencing the direction of the problem-solving.

☐ 6. **Give employees the opportunity to analyze the problem.** By allowing some space, employees can identify alternatives and select a workable, fair solution.

☐ 7. **Encourage employees to research, evaluate, and make recommendations for adaptation.** This will increase motivation, self-direction, and contribution for implementing the change. However, if there are limitations to what can be enacted, be sure to specify them at the onset so that they can be clearly accounted for in the adaptation.

For further information on this topic, order and read:
*Creativity and Business   ***Effective Performance Appraisals, or Personal Performance Contracts
**An Honest Day's Work   ****Effective Meeting Skills
using the list in the back of this book.

Understanding Change

SETTING GOALS AND OBJECTIVES

Once the adaptation phase is underway, you and your employees will need to move into a problem solving/decision making mode. In problem solving/decision making, it is necessary to first clarify and then establish specific goals and objectives. Too frequently people talk in broad terms about wishes and desires. To make things happen you need clearly defined goals and objectives.

CASE STUDY

Mr. and Mrs. Serendipity, owners of the Up & Coming Wholesale Import Company, liked to travel abroad. During their travels they sought merchandise for their company. They preferred not to develop any disciplined group of product. Instead the owners bought what caught their fancy.

Meanwhile, back at home, the sales group worked to the best of their ability to assure customers that whatever Mr. and Mrs. Serendipity found, (whether carpets or china), would surely be a best seller. Requests for catalogs were greeted with a response that the products changed too frequently to justify the cost of printing.

Frequently potential customers turned to other places when they could not find what they wanted even though "Up & Coming" had previously carried it.

What could be done to address this situation?

Did the owners have goals and objectives? Were they in line with planned growth and change for the company?

GOALS AND OBJECTIVES

A GOAL is an overall destination. OBJECTIVES are the points you must reach along the way. For example, a *goal* might be to install a new computer. *Objectives* would include your considerations of cost, performance, software support and so forth.

Goal setting is enhanced when goals are

- publicly committed
- time bound
- contracted

☐ Take time right now to establish three specific goals to use during adaptation to a change at work.

1. _____

2. _____

3. _____

After establishing goals, it is necessary to create objectives for each goal to help you get there. Objectives, as in the computer example, help you to clarify and determine the methods for reaching the goals. Goals and objectives need not be only product or task oriented. Especially during change, it is important to develop people and feeling based goals. Such a goal might be, ''During the move to a new office the stress level in my group will be minimized by extending deadlines on all of the routine reports''.

GOALS AND OBJECTIVES (Continued)

When making objectives, keep in mind the SPIRO model: *Specificity, Performance, Involvement, Realism, Observability* = SPIRO

State **specifically** what your objective is.
Indicate what **performance** level is expected.
Define who must be **involved** in accomplishing it.
Make your objective **realistic**.
Make the accomplishment of your objective **observable**.

Return to the goals you specified above. For each of the goals, specify several objectives. Be sure to use the SPIRO model:

Goal 1: _____

_____

_____

Goal 2: _____

_____

_____

Goal 3: _____

_____

_____

Change requires decisions. Lots of them. Adaptation to change requires goals and objectives. These form a reasonably well-defined map of where you want to go. Without a plan for adapting the changes to the current work environment, muddling through often becomes the dominant strategy. When organizations muddle through, they frequently fail to obtain their goals and objectives. The results can be disastrous. The intended changes do not occur in a productive, economical manner.

PROBLEM SOLVING

With only one objective, the decision is relatively simple. However, when there is more than one objective, you usually must trade-off among the objectives. The trade-offs occur in multiple-objective decisions, because values and vision play important roles. (If you doubt this, think about the last time you bought a car. Did your original goal require any trade-offs insofar as cost, style, timing or performance? How many trade-offs did you make? Did you buy the make and model you dreamed of?)

Just to keep the actual magnitude of your task in perspective, suppose you have 15 objectives and are trying to set priorities. How many ways can this be done? The laws of probability indicate there are approximately 1.3 trillion ways to rank 15 items. No wonder an apparently simple task as setting budget priorities can lead to confusion and sometimes conflict.

As adaptation to the change begins to take place, it is necessary for your employees to develop methods to incorporate these changes into their working lives. Quite frequently they must adapt to new working conditions, policies, product lines, or competitors. Effectively integrating these adaptations becomes a major group priority. Together the employees must effectively solve the problems of adaptation to change.

STRUCTURED GROUP TECHNIQUE

The *structured group technique* is an effective process for group problem solving within groups who are familiar with a particular problem area. When successful adaptation to change requires high group acceptance, it is a particularly helpful problem solving tool.

STRUCTURED GROUP PROBLEM SOLVING ACTIVITY

✔✔TECHNIQUE TO USE

To do a Structured Group Problem Solving process you will need approximately two hours, newsprint/chartpad paper, felt tipped markers for each group, twenty 3x5 cards for each participant, paper & pencil for each participant, masking tape, tables and chairs to accomodate the group.

A. Prior to the Structured Group Problem Solving Session, the leader should write an overview of the problem in the form of a question. (e.g., How can we combine the two marketing staffs into a team?)

_____

_____

B. At your structured group meeting, divide employees into small groups. Appoint a recorder for each group. This person will play a role later.

C. Present each group with the Problem Overview Question. Provide each person in the small group, a blank sheet of paper. (Or you might wish to produce copies of the Problem Overview Question with blank space below for responses). Instruct each group member to *silently, independently, and without discussion* spend fifteen minutes dealing with the problem by writing possible solutions.

STRUCTURED GROUP PROBLEM SOLVING
(Continued)

D. After fifteen minutes, the leader should instruct the groups to ask each group member to present *one* "solution" idea to the group. The recorder lists the idea verbatim on a chartpad, and assigns it a number, in sequence.

E. The process in step D should continue, *without discussion*, until all ideas have been listed.

F. After all ideas have been listed, the group recorder leads the small group to discuss *each* of the ideas in sequence. The purpose of the discussion is to:

   1. clarify
   2. elaborate
   3. evaluate

G. After the discusssion, the recorder should instruct each participant to *individually* select the five best ideas on the list. Each person should put each idea on a 3x5 with it's number from the chartpad.

H. Each participant should then rank the ideas in priority order by assigning a rank order number in the right top corner of the card. (1 = highest priority, 5 = lowest priority)

I. After all members have voted, the recorder should collect the 3x5 cards and tabulate the results on his or her small Group Tally Sheet (shown on the following page). Results can then be shared with the group.

J. Instruct each small group to make a decision based on the outcome of individual member's votes. This decision should be presented to the larger group and form the basis for creating an action plan to **adapt** to the specific change.

STRUCTURED GROUP TALLY SHEET

Item Number   Ranks Assigned   Average of Ranks

_____

_____

_____

_____

_____

_____

_____

_____

_____

_____

_____

_____

_____

_____

_____

_____

Problems with group problem solving:

As you develop problem solving skills in your employees, watch for the following *disadvantages* of group problem-solving. Check any you see occurring in your adaptation process:

☐ Individual domination—one employee filibusters and controls the topic

☐ Social pressure for conformity—employees are afraid to differ with each other

☐ Status incongruities—employee status in the group controls acceptance or rejection of ideas and opinions (i.e., everyone defers to the senior member)

☐ "Self-weighting" effect—employees give more (or less) weight to their own opinions

☐ Premature closure—employees rush to a solution to avoid conflict or debate.

CONFLICT DURING ADAPTATION

As you learned in the last unit, conflict can be a positive force in reaching sound decisions. Sound decisions are the goal of adaptation to change. However, to be a positive force decisions must be made in an atmosphere that encourages the expression of differing opinions.

Your employees must evaluate the consequences of the various alternatives for adapting to a change. They must develop an action plan that allows for maximum productivity and satisfaction of each person. Sometimes this is done individually, more often it is accomplished at the group level.

CONFLICT DURING ADAPTATION (Continued)

When conflict arises in problem solving discussions, three positive factors can emerge:

1. The diverse ideas and perspectives provide a broadened understanding of the nature and implications of the change. Without adequate attention to this phase, there can be backtracking later, because inaccurate assessment and rapid conclusions did not address the *real* problems. The diversity contributes to the adaptation of change at the personal, group and organizational level.

2. The range of different ideas presented gives the group more alternatives for implementing the change. Disagreement is a major contributor to development of alternatives. Without a full range of alternatives, an inappropriate decision may occur.

3. The excitement of conflicting ideas stimulates interaction and involvement with the task. The shared interest that emerges from conflict results in greater creativity, increased commitment to the change, and a higher quality decision. This prepares everyone for the final stage of the change process, namely involvement.

CHANGES CAN BE ABORTED

Don't be surprised, dismayed, and disgruntled if after all your hard work to get the change implemented, it gets aborted. Often, because of the goal setting and problem-solving process during the adaptation stage, unforeseen difficulties with the change emerge. When this occurs and the change is aborted, it is usually for one of the following reasons:

- Unforseen logistic, political or economic problems surface after a lengthly adaptation test phase

- The earlier organizational need that created change no longer exists

- The strategic goals of the organization become modified and don't require the change outcomes

- Key change sponsors or change agents leave the organization or change their minds.

The potential for terminating changes during this phase highlights the importance of the adaptation stage and your role in it. To help you, the following is a review of **adaptation** to change. Adaptation occurs when the following activities are observed. Put a check by any that have occurred in your workplace:

☐ Independence, personal responsibility and acceptance of differences are encouraged.

☐ Acceptance of the change is expressed.

☐ Creative thinking about the change is promoted.

☐ Employees set their own goals for implementation of change.

☐ Employees research, evaluate and make recommendations about implementing changes.

☐ Employees set goals and objectives for accomplishing changes.

☐ Employees participate in decision making about implementing changes.

☐ Employees have a sense of control about their own work.

If you checked at least five, you are well on your way to success!

INCREASING INVOLVEMENT

When you observe that your employees are comfortably in the adaptation stage, it is time to move them to the final stage of change, **involvement**. *Involvement* means overtly supporting solutions designed to implement and install the change. Installation is itself a formal decision to initiate and use the change. It is a commitment to actively invest resources, demonstrate actions and recognize the long range goals that support the change. It often requires you and your employees to subordinate unrelated short-term objectives that are not consistent with the change.

Your job as a change agent is to develop a sense of involvement in all your employees. Once again you should return to the CHANGE MATRIX© (page 44) to evaluate where each employee falls. Do you need to build involvement at the personal level? The group level? Or both? What is the status of the organizational involvement?

If your employees are not committed to the change, their lack of involvement and commitment will most likely cause the change to fail. Ultimately your employees (the change targets), must believe in the change and make a commitment to its implementation.

How can you tell if an employee is involved and committed to a change?

> Commitment occurs when an employee pursues a specific goal in a consistent manner.

INCREASING COMMITMENT INVOLVEMENT
(Continued)

Commitment *and* involvement are *both* necessary for successful installation of a change. To more exactly understand the difference between commitment and involvement, remember the old story about bacon and eggs—the chicken is involved, the pig is committed!

Strategies for involvement and building commitment to a change must be developed and implemented over a period of time. Too often the temptation exists to stop building commitment to the change once it is announced or installed.

Stop and think—How often do you stop your tennis or golf swing at contact with the ball? Adequate follow through is equally important to successfully implement a change.

Too often managers invest considerable time, energy, and money in making a good decision about what to change, but make almost no investment to building involvement and commitment to that decision. That is a mistake. While building involvement and commitment may be expensive, failure to obtain them is more costly. To obtain commitment from your employees you must:

- Provide them with complete and accurate information

- Involve them in the planning and execution of the change

- Reward them for their participation and assistance.

INCREASING INVOLVEMENT AND COMMITMENT (Continued)

The payoff to increasing employee involvement is that they will demonstrate a personal investment to achieve the change. They will be consistent in their actions and reject behaviors and rewards not compatible with implementing the change. They will become advocates for the change, rather than being resistant to it.

TEAM DEVELOPMENT

As involvement with change develops among your employees, so does their sense of teamwork. Your employee group now has a combined sense of purpose and commitment to a common goal. To learn more about developing teamwork with your employees, read *Team Building:* An Exercise In Leadership* by Robert Maddux.

A comparison of teams and groups is shown on the facing page.

☐ Check the characteristics representative of your employees.

GROUPS VS. TEAMS

---

*To order *Team Building,* use the list at the back of this book.

GROUPS VERSUS TEAMS

GROUPS	TEAMS
☐ Members think they are grouped together for administrative purposes only. Individuals work independently; sometimes at cross purposes with others.	☐ Members recognize their inter-dependence and understand both personal and team goals are best accomplished with mutual support. Time is not wasted struggling over "turf" or attempting personal gain at the expense of others.
☐ Members tend to focus on themselves because they are not sufficiently involved in planning the unit's objectives. They approach their job simply as a hired hand.	☐ Members feel a sense of ownership for their jobs and unit because they are committed to goals they helped establish.
☐ Members are told what to do rather than being asked what the best approach would be. Suggestions are not encouraged.	☐ Members contribute to the organization's success by applying their unique talent and knowledge to team objectives.
☐ Members distrust the motives of colleagues because they do not understand the role of other members. Expressions of opinion or disagreement are considered divisive or non-supportive.	☐ Members participate in decisions affecting the team but understand their leader must make a final ruling whenever the team cannot decide, or an emergency exists. Positive results, not conformity are the goal.
☐ Members are so cautious about what they say that real understanding is not possible. Game playing may occur and communications traps may be set to catch the unwary.	☐ Members practice open and honest communication. They make an effort to understand each other's point of view.
☐ Members may receive good training but are limited in applying it to the job by the supervisor or other group members.	☐ Members are encouraged to develop skills and apply what they learn on the job. They receive the support of the team.
☐ Members find themselves in conflict situations which they do not know how to resolve. Their supervisor may put off intervention until serious damage is done.	☐ Members recognize conflict is a normal aspect of human interaction but they view such situations as an opportunity for new ideas and creativity. They work to resolve conflict quickly and constructively.
☐ Members may or may not participate in decisions affecting the team. Conformity often appears more important than positive results.	☐ Members work in a climate of trust and are encouraged to openly express ideas, opinions, disagreements and feelings. Questions are welcomed.

*Adapted from *Team Building: An Exercise in Leadership,* see the list in the back of this book for ordering information.

BE LIKE THE COACH

CASE STUDY

A fast growing corporation wanted to recruit employees who would be flexible and be able to rapidly adapt to the shifting structures created by its growth. For a recruiting model they hired a professional sport's coach known for winning teams. This coach was so good at picking players, his teams won over 80% of their games. How did he do so well when the recruiting draft regulations required him to take low picks because of his winning record year after year?

The coach said he knew exactly what he was looking for when he selected new players. He wanted three things:

1. **An ability to successfully accomplish difficult or unpopular items.**
   He compared an athlete's grades with the subjects that athletes *liked the least.* If the grades were good in those subjects, the coach awarded ''special consideration'' for selection.

2. **The ability to take criticism:** He asked the college coach how eagerly the athlete showed up for some films and how willing the person was to acknowledge mistakes and practice new ways to overcome errors.

3. **The ability to see both the part and the whole of a situation.**
   In a game his players had to know the overall objective of the play. Players had to know their individual parts perfectly. During a game, if a play went awry each player had to know what to do to still meet the objective.

Take a look at your employee group. What can you do to encourage them to demonstrate the flexibility the coach wanted in his players? How can you instill the desire to have your employees work together to successfully implement necessary changes?

ACTIVITIES TO BUILD INVOLVEMENT:

✔✔ TECHNIQUE TO USE

Frequently the task of building involvement during change requires that you give employees an opportunity to explore their personal commitment. The following activities can assist you in this.

Check those activities you plan to use with your employees. I will:

☐ Explore gaps and blockages to individual involvement:
Have everyone talk about how the change will affect them personally.
Listen to their tone. What does it tell you?

☐ Use imagination and fantasy:
Have employees discuss the change from the standpoint of an outsider not directly affected by the change. Observe how that encourages objectivity about the change.

☐ Clarify the unspoken policies:
Have the group turn the change into ''ten commandments'', or ''the word according to...''
Record their answers on a chartpad.

☐ Release the energy blocked by fear by listing responses to:
''I'm afraid the change will:''
or
''I want to see the following result from this change.''

☐ Create roleplays requiring group participation:
''The owner called and told us to get it together or we'd be gone.
To save on jobs we need to...''

THOUGHTS ABOUT THE INVOLVEMENT STAGE

Pessimism can occur during the involvement stage. It is often unavoidable. However, by directly addressing the problems and concerns, everyone's confidence can be increased. Resolving problems occurs best in an environment that encourages all involved to openly discuss their concerns.

It is possible to generate alternative solutions to solve the problems accompanying change. If the employees become involved in the solutions, then their ownership and commitment to the change is increased. As problems are resolved, more realistic levels of conviction begin to emerge. This advances commitment and involvement.

Once a change has been installed and used long enough to demonstrate its worth, the **involvement** stage has worked. Adaptation focused on initial entry problems. Involvement focuses on in-depth, long-term-use considerations. The questions move from ''Can we do it?'' to ''Do we want to continue it?''

In time, a change becomes institutionalized. This occurs once it has a history of worth, durability and continuity. It becomes part of the routine operations of an organization. It is no longer tentative; it becomes the norm. At some future stage it is possible that a change will outlive its usefulness. When this time comes it will require another change cycle. And so it continues with any living organization because the key to survival is a never-ending adaptation to the changing culture and environment.

A FINAL WORD:

When organizational members—change sponsors, agents and targets—commit to change because it fits with their personal interests, goals and value systems, the change becomes internalized. This results in enthusiasm, high-energy, involvement and persistence. At this stage, change sponsors, targets, and agents all are devoted to the task. Each has the ability to engage others in the change effort.

Managing the challenge of change is a powerful responsibility. It is not easy and often it is expensive. However, failing to recognize the need to change and not working to build commitment to the change is far more costly. Making the investment of time, energy and money will benefit everyone: the employee, the management and the organization. Advocates of change will enhance its implementation and installation. And employees will return your investment in them with increased productivity and personal growth.

Remember, you *can* effectively manage change. Moving forward while still preserving desirable aspects of the past is your challenge. You can do it! Good Luck.

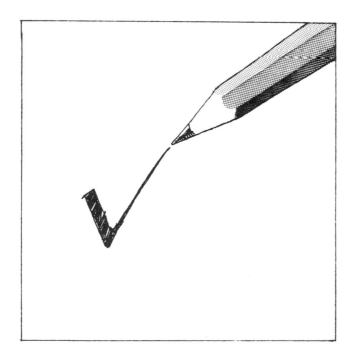

NOTES

NOTES

OVER 150 BOOKS AND 35 VIDEOS AVAILABLE IN THE 50-MINUTE SERIES

We hope you enjoyed this book. If so, we have good news for you. This title is part of the best-selling *50-MINUTE*™ *Series* of books. All *Series* books are similar in size and identical in price. Many are supported with training videos.

To order *50-MINUTE* Books and Videos or request a free catalog, contact your local distributor or Crisp Publications, Inc., 1200 Hamilton Court, Menlo Park, CA 94025. Our toll-free number is (800) 442-7477.

50-Minute Series Books and Videos Subject Areas . . .

Management
Training
Human Resources
Customer Service and Sales Training
Communications
Small Business and Financial Planning
Creativity
Personal Development
Wellness
Adult Literacy and Learning
Career, Retirement and Life Planning

Other titles available from Crisp Publications in these categories

Crisp Computer Series
The Crisp Small Business & Entrepreneurship Series
Quick Read Series
Management
Personal Development
Retirement Planning